Christmas Therapy

Christmas Therapy

written by
Karen Katafiasz

illustrated by
R.W. Alley

ABBEY PRESS

© 1994 by St. Meinrad Archabbey
Published by Abbey Press
St. Meinrad, Indiana 47577

All rights reserved.
No part of this book may be used or reproduced in any manner
without written permission of the publisher, except in the case of
brief quotations embodied in critical articles and reviews.

Library of Congress Catalog Number
93-073804

ISBN 0-87029-268-4

Printed in the United States of America

Foreword

Have you ever promised yourself at Christmas that *next* year the holidays would be less frenzied and more meaningful? Then next year comes, the Yule treadmill starts up again, and you find yourself jumping on board as always.

Or maybe difficult or disappointing experiences have diminished your hope for a Christmas that's truly merry. And so you drag yourself through the season with a cynical "humbug!" and little joy.

Either way, by New Year's you can end up feeling depleted, inadequate, and empty.

Maybe it's time for some gentle, constructive, self-help therapy—*Christmas Therapy.*

Here you'll find do-able suggestions for eliminating excess and unreasonable expectations, while you maintain the best of holiday traditions and keep yourself balanced.

Alive-with-color pages evoke the magic and exuberance, the wonder and enchantment that can make your spirit soar during this glorious time.

Most importantly, you're invited to reflect—within your own heart, in your own way—on the event at the center of the celebration. For it's there that the essential, most profound Christmas therapy lies: in the meaning and mystery of Jesus' birth.

1.

Christmas is more than a deadline or a day on the calendar. It is a journey of the spirit—from darkness to light, from chaos to peace, from separateness to the union of love.

2.

In this season of lights, enjoy
the external sparkle. And then
let that outer radiance point you
to the inner Light of Christmas
that dwells in your own heart.

3.

Christmas is God's feast for the senses! Observe its shimmering sights, inhale its aromatic smells, hear its resonating sounds, savor its delectable tastes, feel its enticing textures.

4.

You don't have to fulfill others'
expectations about what
Christmas should be. Consider
whether your plans and
preparations will enhance your
celebration or whether they're
only a response to family or
cultural pressures. Free yourself
to create a more meaningful
observance.

5.

Don't tie yourself to traditions that have become more chores than cherished rituals. Traditions are enriching when they allow the past to inspire and inspirit the present. Shape your traditions according to your needs and values now.

6.

Simplify your celebration. Big is not always best. Expensive is not always valuable. Time-consuming is not always lasting.

7.

Decorate your home with meaning and purpose and joy. Let something of your own and your family history be told in the decorations.

8.

Relish the expectancy of the season, the delicious tension of anticipation. Stay in the moment and experience it completely; wait mindfully.

9.

Make time for your favorite expressions of Christmas lore, like treasured music, stories, poems, and films. Reflect on their changing meaning for you over the years.

10.

Relinquish superhuman efforts to produce Christmas-card-perfect holiday celebrations. Christmas is about God becoming human—not humans becoming gods.

11.

Relinquish expectations for holidays that are without conflict or problems or challenges. Christmas is about God embracing human life—with all its shortcomings, mistakes, and struggles.

12.

When the season's commercialism becomes too oppressive, place yourself in spirit in the simple and earthy surroundings of Jesus' birth. Remind yourself what really matters.

13.

If gift-giving has taken on a sense of tiresome obligation, explore ways to refresh its meaning. Talk over with family and friends how to better reflect God's gift of love to us all.

14.

Enhance your Christmas-card correspondence by taking time to add a special note to each person on your list. As you write to your loved ones, hold them prayerfully in your heart.

15.

Allow yourself adequate rest, exercise, and nourishment each day. These lasting gifts to yourself will help you to maintain your balance, energy, and inner peace throughout the season.

16.

When the whirlwind of activity becomes too great, find the silent night in your heart. Promise yourself that you'll return there whenever you need to.

17.

Take care of yourself during holiday family gatherings. Sometimes family togetherness doesn't feel good because of negative patterns that started long ago. Stay centered and detach yourself from old unhealthy behavior.

18.

Spend time with children.
Relish their delight; experience
their wide-eyed expectation. If
disappointment, pain, or
cynicism has crushed your own
expectation, give it new life.

19.

During this time of enchantment and anticipation for children, reflect on the child within you. What does your inner child especially cherish about this season? What gifts would your child within like to have?

20.

Remember how you experienced Christmas as a child. If that child was hurt or wounded, be a loving parent to that child now; provide needed healing.

21.

Cherish your joyful memories of Christmases past. Tell others about them; re-create them with loved ones when you can.

22.

If this Christmas season is not all it was in former years, remember that in God's time all the joy and wonder of the past are present in this moment too. Happiness once experienced is yours forever.

23.

When death or distance or
circumstance separates you from
loved ones, keep them close in
thought. You may want to
celebrate a ritual in their honor
or change your familiar routine
to ease the pain.

24.

If you hurt this Christmas,
know that you are not alone.
Experience the reality of
"Emmanuel," which means
"God with us."

25.

If you hurt this Christmas,
know that you are not alone. To
live fully means sometimes to be
in pain; you share a sacred bond
with others who are also
hurting.

26.

Find a way to reach out to those who are hurting this Christmas. Visit nursing home residents, deliver food baskets, welcome someone who's alone into your home.

27.

Christmas is God's affirmation of the goodness of being human. Honor the sacredness of your own humanity by experiencing life deeply and passionately.

28.

Christmas is a time to touch hands and touch hearts. Offer love, acceptance, and peace to those around you.

29.

Believe in the magic of Christmas: children's hugs, unexpected snowfalls, strangers' greetings, unwarranted acts of kindness. Store the magic in your heart all year long.

30.

Believe in the meaning of
Christmas: divine love
embracing the world, the
longing toward Infinity, life
infused with Mystery. Store the
meaning in your soul all year
long.

Karen Katafiasz is books and programs director at Abbey Press. She is the author of *Celebrate-your-womanhood Therapy* and the editor of *Grief Therapy*. A native of Toledo, Ohio, she now lives—appropriately—on Prancer Drive in Santa Claus, Indiana.

Illustrator for the Abbey Press Elf-help Books, **R.W. Alley** also illustrates and writes children's books. He lives in Barrington, Rhode Island, with his wife, daughter, and son.

The Story of the Abbey Press Elves

The engaging figures that populate the Abbey Press "elf-help" line of publications and products first appeared in 1987 on the pages of a small self-help book called *Be-good-to-yourself Therapy*. Shaped by the publishing staff's vision and defined in R.W. Alley's inventive illustrations, they lived out author Cherry Hartman's gentle, self-nurturing advice with charm, poignancy, and humor.

Reader response was so enthusiastic that more Elf-help Books were soon under way, a still-growing series that has inspired a line of related gift products.

The especially endearing character featured in the early books—sporting a cap with a mood-changing candle in its peak—has since been joined by a spirited female elf with flowers in her hair.

These two exuberant, sensitive, resourceful, kindhearted, lovable sprites, along with their lively elfin community, reveal what's truly important as they offer messages of joy and wonder, playfulness and co-creation, wholeness and serenity, the miracle of life and the mystery of God's love.

With wisdom and whimsy, these little creatures with long noses demonstrate the elf-help way to a rich and fulfilling life.

**Elf-help Books . . . adding "a little character"
and a lot of help to self-help reading!**

Christmas Therapy
#20175-6 $5.95   ISBN 0-87029-268-4

Grief Therapy
#20178-0 $3.95   ISBN 0-87029-267-6

More Be-good-to-yourself Therapy
#20180-6 $3.95   ISBN 0-87029-262-5

Happy Birthday Therapy
#20181-4 $3.95   ISBN 0-87029-260-9

Acceptance Therapy Deluxe Edition
#20182-2 $5.95   ISBN 0-87029-259-5

Forgiveness Therapy
#20184-8 $3.95   ISBN 0-87029-258-7

Keep-life-simple Therapy
#20185-5 $3.95   ISBN 0-87029-257-9

Be-good-to-your-body Therapy
#20188-9 $3.95   ISBN 0-87029-255-2

Celebrate-your-womanhood Therapy
#20189-7 $3.95   ISBN 0-87029-254-4

Acceptance Therapy
#20190-5 $3.95   ISBN 0-87029-245-5

Keeping-up-your-spirits Therapy
#20195-4 $3.95   ISBN 0-87029-242-0

Play Therapy
#20200-2 $3.95   ISBN 0-87029-233-1

Slow-down Therapy
#20203-6 $3.95   ISBN 0-87029-229-3

One-day-at-a-time Therapy
#20204-4 $3.95   ISBN 0-87029-228-5

(Book list continued on next page.)

**Elf-help Books . . . adding "a little character"
and a lot of help to self-help reading!**

Prayer Therapy
#20206-9 $3.95   ISBN 0-87029-225-0

Be-good-to-your-marriage Therapy
#20205-1 $3.95   ISBN 0-87029-224-2

Be-good-to-yourself Therapy
#20255-6 $3.95   ISBN 0-87029-209-9

Available at your favorite bookstore or directly from us at
Abbey Press Publications, St. Meinrad, IN 47577.
Phone orders: Call 1-800-325-2511.